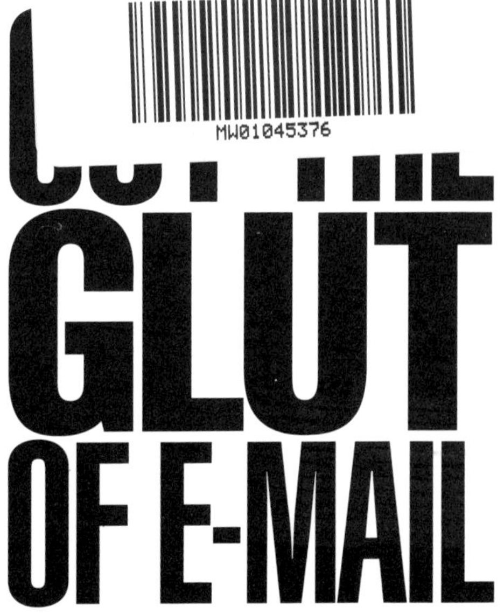


## Solving the in-box problem from outside the box

**Mark Ellwood**

Published by Pace Productivity Inc.
Toronto, Canada

Published by:

Pace Productivity Inc.
350 Sunnyside Avenue
Toronto, Ontario, Canada
M6R 2R6

Canadian Cataloguing in Publication Data

Ellwood, Mark 1956–
Cut the glut of e-mail: solving the in-box problem from outside the box

ISBN 0-9682395-2-8

1. Electronic mail systems. I. Title.

HE7551.E42 2002 004.692 C2001-904035-0

Edited and typeset by Colborne Communications
Cover design by Public Image Design
Photograph by David Bidner
Technical review by Wally Gross and William Stratas

Printed and bound in Canada by Webcom Limited

Fan support from Doug West and hugs from Susan

# TABLE OF CONTENTS

# INTRODUCTION

"I'm just swamped with e-mail." Who would have thought that just a few years back, e-mail would create the kind of exasperation you hear so much of these days? E-mail promised a world of instant communication and better productivity. To some extent, that has occurred. What used to take days to deliver now only takes minutes, if that. But like any technology, e-mail has also created unexpected spin-offs, like misunderstood mailings, confusing correspondence, unnecessary messages, and unsolicited pitches. Ironically, despite all of these negative side effects, people panic when the e-mail system breaks down for just a few hours.

Today, complaining about e-mail is a badge of honor. People talk about the volume of e-mail they receive as if they're boasting about battle wounds: "Our platoon slogged through 20 miles of swamp last night. Then we hit the land mines. We lost five men and I got a piece of shrapnel from a booby trap lodged in my leg. The bugs are eating us alive, we haven't had a solid meal for three days, and I received 112 e-mails this morning. If I can answer the e-mails and get past the snipers, I think we'll make it."

Are co-workers being resentful or boastful when they return from a vacation and comment on the glut of e-mails cramming their in-basket? Pity the poor soul who returns from a four-day sickness and discovers only three e-mails in the in-basket: a list of the weekly cafeteria specials, a reminder to donate a share to the department's weekly lottery ticket pool, and a note from the boss that an e-mail from the week before requires a response.

People complain about e-mail as if a horde of evil aliens were hurling a volley of missives at them. But take a moment and answer these two questions: 1) Do you receive a lot of e-mail that you shouldn't? Probably yes. 2) Do you send a lot of e-mail that you shouldn't? Probably no.

But wait a minute. If you're not the culprit, then who is? Everyone else? There is no "everyone else." "They" are not the ones who are causing the glut of e-mail – you are. The truth is that everyone must take responsibility for the glut of e-mail. Including you.

This book is designed to provide simple and unconventional techniques for reducing the glut of e-mail you receive and send. You won't find technical descriptions, lists of web sites, or references to specific products, since they can quickly become outdated. What you will find are simple suggestions for changes you can make largely on your own. If you're not sure how to implement some of the ideas, explore the features on your e-mail system. Take another look at the properties, preferences, and options to learn what will work on your system. Use the "help" feature to guide you. You can discover features you hadn't seen before. Also, get to know your system administrator, or your computer consultant. He or she can help you, but you have to ask first.

When you read these tips, your immediate reaction might be one of skepticism. You may think, "These tips sound nice, but they wouldn't work in my company." If that's the case, remind yourself that when your e-mails pile up, your productivity goes down. You can't just wish away e-mail. Dramatic changes are needed.

The content of this book comes out of the productivity research we've conducted in recent years. As part of our consulting and training practice, we conduct time studies for clients. In a recent project, Helen, a vice president at a major bank, discovered she spends over seven hours per week on unnecessary e-mail. That doesn't include all the legitimate correspondence that she measured separately!

Results like these occur because a series of conventions, rules, and procedures have evolved around e-mail that can be highly unproductive. Not only are tips needed, but so is a change in thinking about how people use this relatively new medium. You can make that change. Challenge the conventions. Break the rules. Change the procedures. Be bold and take action. Your time is worth it.

# REDUCE THE E-MAIL YOU RECEIVE

## Turn off the notification function

It's Wednesday morning and you're working on an important project. You're at your computer revising a document, entering data into a spreadsheet, or reviewing notes from a conversation with an important contact. Then you hear a distinctive "ping!" and a familiar icon pops up to announce that you have a new e-mail. So you open the message, only to discover that you've been copied on a note about something of no importance. Delete. Now, back to work. Where were you?

Interruptions like these sap your productivity. For example, Antonia, an employee at a large financial services company, suffered doubly from this annoying notification function, also known as a "break" feature. First, her computer was not equipped with speakers. So when new e-mails arrived, she didn't hear an audible signal. Then, the system jammed her keyboard until she acknowledged the message. Antonia found herself typing at length without looking at her screen, only to discover that her typing was no longer registering. She had to retype a portion of her work after dealing with the incoming e-mail.

If your e-mail system is set up to interrupt you this way, you're losing time and productivity. When you're involved with a major project, you need concentration to complete your high-priority tasks. Don't let e-mails distract you at random. Change the settings of your system or ask your system administrator to change them. Disable the notification function and answer e-mails at reasonably periodic intervals – chosen by you, not your computer.

Do you rush to answer the doorbell while helping your children with homework? Are you one of those people who grabs a ringing phone while eating dinner? If so, you're likely the type who's tempted to open your e-mail as soon as it arrives. Remember that nothing stunning is likely to have arrived. There are no announcements that you've just won a million dollars or invitations to dine with the secretary-general of the United Nations. It's just e-mail.

So avoid the rush response. Stick to doing what you *should* be doing and block off time to answer your e-mail later. The world won't end if you don't get to it right away. Consider whose schedule you want to live by, your own or everyone else's?

## Hire someone to go through your e-mail

Remember secretaries? They used to type letters, sort mail, reserve flights, greet visitors, answer phones, arrange meetings, and take messages. Now, almost nobody has a secretary. Technology has replaced them. But many of the clerical tasks they handled still need to be done, so managers find themselves doing more and more "administrivia."

It's time to bring back secretaries – people who are experts at day-to-day administration. Unfortunately, managers often feel that having fewer people saves money. As a partner at a large consulting firm said, "Remember, we started as an accounting firm, and the accountants see extra people as extra costs." This kind of thinking doesn't recognize the massive hidden costs of managers spending time conducting routine tasks. Deleting unnecessary e-mail is one of these tasks.

So hire an assistant, share one with a group of managers, or employ a student as a part-time assistant who could work from home. You don't need a full-time employee, just someone who can spend an hour per day to save you valuable time.

If you have a web master or computer consultant, he or she can also help with screening. One form of screening uses applications that "peek" into your mail server account without actually downloading the messages. The administrative assistant can identify unsolicited messages and delete them directly off the server, before the executive calls up his or her mail each morning.

The biggest objection to this is the fear of compromising confidentiality. However, this is not an issue, as secretaries are experts at dealing with confidential items. With appropriate direction, your assistant will know how to deal with your e-mail. He or she will be interested in getting through it quickly, not digesting it all.

Provide your assistant with a clear set of guidelines. Some files can be thrown out, others can be rerouted to particular boxes, and others can be summarized. This is what secretaries used to do. Smart managers will bring back the practice. Perhaps you can't get permission? If you're on a bonus system, calculate what improving your productivity would be worth by hiring someone out of your own pocket. How much more income could you generate as a result? Don't think like an accountant, think like an entrepreneur.

## Don't accept messages from on-line groups

Stamp collectors unite! Just visit an on-line newsgroup or discussion group where you can share ideas, queries, and information with others who have similar interests. (Newsgroups are generally accessible to anyone, whereas a discussion group usually involves a sign-up procedure.) These groups allow you to "post" a message to a central board that's accessible to all of the other group members. Perhaps you need help figuring out a feature of your software program. Or maybe you're looking for a vendor for a particular type of service, or you have an opinion about a book that you've read. On-line groups put you in touch with others quickly.

When you see a subject of interest, you can post your own response. You would do this to help someone out or to provide a point of view. On the other hand, if you're a bit on the shy side, you don't have to post anything. You can simply read all of the messages left by others. This is curiously known as "lurking."

You can participate by logging on to a newsgroup or visiting a discussion group's web site. Some groups will also send you all of the postings by e-mail. If the group is popular, you'll be overwhelmed by a glut of posts in no time. Chances are many of them will be of little interest.

Instead of receiving all of the posts, disable this function. The newsgroup or discussion group will have a feature that allows you to do this. Look under the set up page or the account status manager. If not, you can set up a filter on your own system to prevent messages from reaching you.

If you want to post a note or review those from others, go to the web site or discussion group where you can see all of the posts in one spot. Pick a time once a day or once a week to go there and review them. In this way, you control what you want to see rather than allowing the groups to control you.

By the way, do not forward personal e-mail to a discussion group without the author's permission. Also, instead of attaching files when posting, refer participants to a web site where they can find the information. And don't send entire web pages, just the web site address. Finally, don't blatantly promote your business. Netiquette rules, or Internet manners, are just common sense.

## Prevent spam

There are few things more unwanted in life than blocked toilets. Spam might be one of them. Spam is unsolicited, commercial e-mail. Savvy marketers use software robot applications to "mine" web sites, discussion groups, and e-mail systems, by collecting e-mail addresses embedded in the page text and scripts. (These software robot applications work similarly to search engine robots that read and index web pages.) There is a thriving sub-industry selling CD-ROMs of millions of harvested e-mail addresses, including yours. With these addresses, potentially hundreds of marketers can send you e-mail. The way to prevent unsolicited e-mail promotions is to prevent the marketers from getting your e-mail address.

- Beware of filling out forms. On some web sites, filling out an on-line form is the only way you can get information or receive an order confirmation. If the site conforms to professional practices, it should post a privacy statement, an address and a phone number. In this case, you are probably safe in submitting your e-mail address. The site may also have a box you can check, asking if it's all right to "send occasional information about products and services that might be of interest." This is a nice way for the marketer to ask if it's OK to send you a lot of advertisements. Check the box that says "no."
- Change your "from" address when you post a note to a discussion group. Some participants do this so their real e-mail address won't work when marketing companies automatically mine it. For instance, the address might read james@NOSPAM.xxyz.com. When you want someone to respond, you instruct

people to remove the "NOSPAM" part when they send a return e-mail. This technique is clunky and not always effective. The smart spammers can find out your real address behind this, but you can use this technique to ward off some of them.

- Don't send back warranty cards, unless you want to receive updates about new products. If you want to avoid getting extra correspondence, either by snail mail or e-mail, don't bother. The chances of most products being defective are pretty slim to begin with. In the rare case that your product has a manufacturer's defect, the manufacturer will honor the warranty based on a sales receipt. Consumer law is based on date of purchase and does not require a registration to provide warranty service.
- Cloak your e-mail address on your web site. An easy way for the spammers' robots to harvest your e-mail address occurs when it appears on your web site. Ask your web master to cloak the embedded e-mail address with special characters and scripts that are known to defeat spam robots. If he or she doesn't know how to do this, ask around and find someone who does.
- Set up a special e-mail address on your web site for general information requests. All the unwanted mail will go there, instead of going directly to your personal e-mail account.
- When submitting your web site to search engines, avoid free services offering to conduct submissions for you. These companies are in the business of harvesting e-mail addresses and many search engines

will block them out. Hire a professional to submit your site to search engines.

- Never respond to a spammer by hitting the reply button. Also, the bottom of a spammer's e-mail often offers you a way to opt out by returning the e-mail with "remove" in the subject header. This is simply a way for your address to be verified so it can be sold to others. Don't bother.

## Avoid free directories

Nothing in life is free. So avoid signing up with directories. There are free services that allow you to update your personal information on various directories for high schools, university groups, etc. One of them encourages you to:

> add your free listing to our e-mail address directory to create your personalized presence in cyberspace. Expand your current listing to include your personal interests, school, group affiliations, and more. Add your personal home page to the largest collections of categorized home pages of people from around the world....

Now why would companies want all that information for free? They want to turn you into a new customer, of course. Don't fall for it.

Another service offers free web e-mail. You can have your e-mail forwarded to a web site and be able to access your messages from anywhere in the world. Thus, when you're in London, you don't have to pay long-distance charges to dial your e-mail host in Atlanta. Sounds good, but it isn't. The web site's privacy section mentions that e-mail is "private correspondence between the sender and the recipient. It is our policy to respect the privacy of visitors." Then it goes on to list three exceptions to this policy. Nowhere does it mention that the actual e-mail address is private. As a result, your e-mail address can be sold to advertisers. Remember the cardinal rule: nothing is free.

## Choose a permanent e-mail address

Whenever you change your e-mail address, you end up creating confusion and a glut of e-mail. Let's say you discontinue an address because you change jobs. Or perhaps you changed your name when you got married, or subscribed with a new service provider when you moved to a new city. If you can foresee one of these events, perhaps you can choose an e-mail address that won't change. For instance, you can establish a personal domain name and address that would be immune to change.

Otherwise, here's what could happen. Stacy Adams sends you an e-mail, requesting the name of a colleague you both knew from high school. The service provider can no longer find you, so it sends the e-mail back to Stacy with an "undeliverable message" response. Stacy tries again anyway and gets the same response. So she e-mails her friend Howard

Goodman, who says he doesn't know where you are, but perhaps you could try Angelo Romano. But when Stacy tries Angelo, she gets an autoresponse from him saying he's away on holidays. The story goes on. The e-mails pile up. Choose your address wisely. Assume it's for life.

If you really must change your address, send out your notification from your new address. Here's an example of an actual e-mail sent a little before its time:

> AABC service is no longer providing support for my computer operating system, NT 4.0, so I have to change to XXYZ provider. My new address is: James@XXYZprovider.com.

This looks appropriate enough. But if a recipient of this note were to hit the reply button, the response would be sent to the old address at AABC provider. Wait until you officially switch your address before sending out a note.

---

## Be less available

Show-offs get all the e-mail they don't want. If you're always showing off by demonstrating how available you are to respond, then people will take you up on your offer. If they know you're always checking your mail on your way to work, at lunch, going home, on a weekend, late at night, or on vacation, then they'll send you more. The more available you are, the more people will try to be in touch with you.

Cellular phones are now equipped with features that let you accept e-mail anywhere. Why anyone would want to read a lengthy document on a screen the size of business card is difficult to understand. And why they would want to do it while driving to work on a busy highway is beyond comprehension. But people do. They feel that if they're not available all the time, they're missing something. They certainly are. They're missing balance, peace, family time and solitude – what most people crave more of.

Making yourself constantly available is ultimately a no-win situation. You simply can't be available all the time, and there is no reason you should. Frustration is growing with cell phones ringing in restaurants, in movie theatres, on the golf course, and in seminars. Surely somewhere there's an upset spouse whose amorous intentions have been interrupted by an unwanted call. "Just let me get this honey. It'll just take a minute...."

People display their status by showing that they're constantly in demand. But ask people about status when a persistent ring is interrupting you. They won't say, "I'm really impressed at how important you are when you get all those calls and e-mails." If you ask them for the honest truth, they would say, "I don't feel important when you interrupt what we're doing to take those calls. I'm not impressed. I *am* impressed when you ignore all that stuff and focus your attention on me!"

Receiving e-mail on the fly isn't much different from receiving calls. When you're going out for dinner, spending time with your family, getting fit, or taking a vacation, that's what you should be concentrating on. So make yourself less available.

## Screen with filters

Block the spammers! They're the marketers who find your e-mail address through the Internet and send you unsolicited e-mail. If your corporate system isn't blocking them, or if you're getting a lot of junk e-mail at home, you can set up filters within your desktop e-mail application. Just like an air filter that blocks unwanted contaminants, e-mail filters block out unwanted spam by sending them to a trash folder.

One tool is the "block sender" function of your e-mail program. Look for this function in the "message rules" section. It will divert mail to a delete file, or prevent it from being downloaded from your server.

Another filter technique is to block key words. Set your filter to screen specific words or phrases such as when both "earn" and "$" appear in a subject line. Or you can delete everything with the word "FREE." If it's free, there could be a catch. And if there's a catch, you're not interested.

Most people who block key words do so in subject lines. When you block words in the text, you run the risk of blocking a message that you want. Wally, an Internet consultant, discovered to his dismay that he had lost out on a bid he had submitted to a prospective client. In his bid, he mentioned that he would be using an open source product that was near the commercial stage and therefore free at the time, which would save the client substantially. Unfortunately, the client never received the bid because he had blocked all incoming e-mail with the word "free" in the text. Having said that, many spam e-mails contain common phrases that could be effectively used as filters – "Bill S.1618" (referring to a federal law regarding unsolicited e-mail), "to be removed from," and "reply with remove."

You can also create a filter by sending all incoming mail with your proper e-mail address on it to a specially-named folder. Call this folder "Priority Mail" or something similar. Everything else, including mail to undisclosed recipients (which is often junk), will end up in your main in-box. This doesn't eliminate any unwanted mail. It simply separates most of it for easier reviewing and deleting.

Filtering, as described above, can only go so far. Like any security system, if the bad guys want to get in, they'll find a way. At least you can weed out the amateurs. To stop the pros, the best filter is to block the originating server. Many of them have to broadcast from their own servers because no Internet service provider would allow them to maintain an account. Ask your Internet service provider, system administrator, or computer consultant to help you weed them out.

## Say "no" to newsletters

You don't need any more newsletters. If you're on a mailing list for which you have no interest, reply by typing "unsubscribe" or "remove" in the comment box, or send a note to the sender telling him or her to stop sending you newsletters.

How do you know which newsletters you should discontinue? Probably all of them. The vast majority of free newsletters are essentially sales brochures disguised as useful information. Most of the information is available elsewhere. Whether it's daily health tips or stock market advice, an e-mail newsletter is not likely to be your best source of information.

Perhaps you find yourself saying, "I receive that newsletter because I might need it sometime." Basing your decisions about self-development on the chance that you might benefit at some undetermined time is foolish. The same goes for subscription newsletters you receive by e-mail. Ask yourself how often you're referring to them. If you're not reading them, you should stop subscribing to them. Otherwise, they'll just take up room needlessly.

## Schedule your instant messaging

Instant messaging can remove hurdles and speed up headaches. E-mail is known as an asynchronous medium. This means that when you send a message, it doesn't appear instantly at the other end. It gets routed through a number of servers, bundled up with other messages along the way, rerouted a couple of times, delivered to a server, then downloaded to a desktop. So a message can take a while to transmit – usually somewhere between a few seconds and a few hours.

Instant messaging is just what it sounds like. You and someone else are on-line at the same time. With the help of your instant messaging software, you can type a note that appears instantly on the other person's screen. You can communicate with one or many people. Whole groups can stay in touch with each other in a virtual chat room.

A few years ago, IBM adopted instant messaging internally. *Fast Company Magazine* reported on the Chief Information Officer's enthusiasm for it: "People think nothing of messaging me," says the CIO. "That technology lets me reach down several levels in the company, and it lets others reach up. It's an important tool that allows me to sniff out a problem quickly." That's curious. Isn't that what the telephone was supposed to do? Here's an organization that has replaced a perfectly good medium, the phone, with one that is not as good. However fast instant messaging is, it can't express tone of voice, and it's only as fast as a typist's fingers. Who knows? Perhaps the next step backwards will be people sending Morse code to each other. (In fact, they already do. Ever see kids sending coded text messages on their phones?)

Instant messaging will bog you down when your friends want to reach you at work. On the other hand, it's an excellent collaborative tool. For project teams, instant contact facilitates discussion. Be sure to schedule those sessions, and have an agenda for what you want to do. Accept no interruptions while you're in a virtual discussion. You wouldn't want your mother walking into a meeting to invite you to dinner on Sunday. Your instant messaging sessions should not be any different.

## Reduce the number of accounts

Communication technology keeps giving people more and more ways to be out of touch with each other. How many times have you called someone, only to hear a voice message encouraging you to reach him or her on a cell phone? That sounds like a pretty good alternative, you figure. So you call the cell phone and get another voice mail message. What's the point? The way to manage your communications is to have fewer ways for people to get in touch with you. The same is true for e-mail addresses. If you work for a company, you can have a work-assigned address. That's the one that changes when you change jobs. And you likely have a home e-mail address for family, friends, and your local interest group. Don't add any more or you'll find the job of managing multiple addresses overly time-consuming. Less is more.

# HANDLE YOUR E-MAIL SMARTLY

## Block off times for e-mail

Lots of e-mail is just plain junk, but all of it needs to be dealt with. Instead of taking care of it when it arrives, which can be disruptive, deal with it on your terms, and on your own time.

Before you open your e-mail in the morning, take a few minutes to plan your day. Start your planning by imagining a completely blank slate. Your day is a void. You have nothing at all to do: no e-mails, phone calls, meetings, interruptions, or reports. Nothing. Then, ask yourself the question, "If I had nothing to do today, what would I do to affect my results one month from now?" This means tackling long-term projects, like planning next year's budget, setting up sales appointments, recruiting a new employee, designing a marketing campaign, or investigating a new software system. Also, ask yourself what you could finish today. Formulating the entire year's budget isn't possible in a day. However, you could review results from last year, design a brief survey to send out to stakeholders, or schedule a meeting for your team. Block off time for these high-priority activities.

After the "A" priorities come the "B" responsibilities, which are the activities from your job description that must get done today. For managers, this might mean creating a staff schedule or updating management on your results. For sales reps, it might mean making sales calls or providing customer service. And for trainers, activities might include making room arrangements. Tackle these in order of priority. You can also block off time for some of these.

Next come the "C" requirements. These are the tasks that are required of you: paperwork, staff meetings, filling out expense reports, travel, and yes, responding to a lot of e-mail. Some of your e-mail deals with your high-priority tasks while much of it is essentially low-priority administrative work. Your "C" requirements can be scheduled too, but only after you've planned for the higher priority "As" and "Bs." So check your e-mail less frequently than you do now. Avoid the temptation. There may not be much of interest anyway.

## Sort your incoming messages

How do you sort a stack of paper mail when it arrives? Do you put a piece over here and another over there? This other one? Maybe you'll look at it later. You take one big stack and sort it into smaller stacks, then accumulate all of those into one big pile. Casino dealers only wish they could shuffle so well.

Reduce your sorting time and you'll increase your efficiency. The same goes for e-mail. Sort by sender, subject line, date, or even receiver if you have more than one e-mail address. In this way, you can process related mail together. Linda, who works at a large bank, sorts her messages in chronological order. When she receives a few notes from one sender, she opens the most recent one first. In this way, she picks up the gist of the previous notes, without having to go through them all.

Just like with traditional snail mail, there are only four things you can do with e-mail as it arrives. A handy acronym known as FLAG is a useful reminder. "F" stands for "file." This means moving it to a file, to be accessed later. The file might be for reference or for follow-up. If you open a note, read it, then say, "Let's see, I'll do something about this later on," you're breaking the FLAG rule. File the note into a folder marked "To be done," or "Upcoming events," or even "Projects in progress." Reading an e-mail and doing nothing is a waste of time.

"L" stands for "let someone else do it." Forward the note to a subordinate, another department, or an associate. Include a short note on top and delegate what you want done.

"A" means "take action." Write a response, make a phone call, or solve a problem. Taking action also includes writing down an item to be done tomorrow, or scheduling an event in your daily planner.

Finally, "G" means "throw it in the garbage." Delete it. If you're afraid that you might need to keep something "just in case," then put it into a file labeled "Delete later." Purge this file periodically.

## Create form letters

Ever find yourself writing the same response over and over again? Someone e-mails you with a request for pricing, membership information, or product features.

Or perhaps someone wants to complain about a product, or submit a resume for a job. Each time, you compose a new response, writing variations of standard sentences as you go. Anytime you're repeating a clerical task is an appropriate time to automate.

First, you can prevent these queries by adding more information to your web site. But the queries will still come in. One option is to create a standard response on your word processing system then cut and paste it into an e-mail response. Remember to add a bit of personalization. Address the person by name, and add a sentence or two at the beginning that relates to his or her question.

Another way to create a form letter is to use a series of different signature files. Signatures at the bottom of e-mails show your name and phone number. Lengthen this part, so it becomes an entire form letter. If your e-mail system allows them, create two or three different signatures to respond to different types of queries. Personalize a short response at the beginning and attach the signature file with the standard, detailed information needed.

Your e-mail system may also allow you to create "stationery." Explore the message features where, depending on your system, you'll discover preloaded graphics for birthday and holiday announcements. This feature also lets you create your own stationery. Skip the goofy graphics though, and insert your form letter into a blank e-mail. Be sure to personalize your letters when you send them out. Use technology to reduce your clerical time, instead of adding to it.

## Delegate instead of doing it

E-mails will bog you down because everyone has an excuse for not delegating them. Here are some of the common excuses:

- I could do it better myself.
- I don't know if I can trust her to do it.
- He isn't qualified to do it.
- She doesn't want any added responsibilities.
- I don't have the time to show anyone how to do it.
- There is no one else to delegate to.
- He already has enough to do.
- I don't want to give up this task because I like doing it.
- I'm the only person who knows how to do this.
- She messed up last time, so I'm not giving her anything else to do.

All of these statements are unfounded. There *is* someone else to delegate to, and they *will* do a good job, if you handle the delegation properly.

First, assume that most people want added responsibilities. (Don't you?) Assume they are keen to learn and take on new tasks. They might even do a better job than you by developing an innovative methodology. If they're not entirely ready, they'll need some training and direction. That's a short-term investment that will pay off many times in the end.

Who can you delegate to? Look around. Even though you're not the boss, there are people who will help if you approach them in the right way. For a salesperson, this can be someone in the customer service department. For a self-employed researcher, it can be a spouse, child, or a neighbor.

What should you delegate? Get help with routine activities such as fact-finding assignments, problem analysis, data collection, photocopying, printing, and travel arrangements. Delegate things that aren't part of your core competency. For small businesses, these include accounting, web site design, deliveries, hardware upkeep, software help, graphic design, travel arrangements, patenting, legal issues, and payroll. However, you can't delegate some things: performance reviews, discipline, firing, and praise.

Create a plan to delegate but don't give out assignments haphazardly. Someone else can do the task, but you're still responsible for the completion of it, and for managing the delegation process.

## Provide clear direction

Tomorrow's forecast is for e-mail flurries. When tasks aren't clearly defined, the notes go back and forth. You can prevent the deluge by getting your message right the first time. Clarify the task you delegate by making sure the standards and the outcome are understood. Explain what needs to be done, when it should be finished, and to what degree of detail. Then ask, "Is there anything else you need to get started?" The person you have delegated the task to will let you know if he or she needs more guidance, or a demonstration of your technique. If not, you can leave the person on his or her own. Only do a checkup at the next benchmark step you've both agreed on.

These steps are done awkwardly via e-mail, so delegate in person. E-mail is an appropriate way to get updates, ask for progress reports, set interim deadlines, and obtain feedback. Simply asking, "How's it going with that new project?" should suffice.

As well, be sure to delegate to the right person. Don't always give tasks to the strongest, most experienced, or first available person. Spread delegation around and give people new experiences as part of their training. When you do, delegate the authority along with the responsibility. Don't make people come back to you for too many minor approvals. Then trust people to do their best and don't check up with them between updates, unless they ask.

When the task is completed, give praise and feedback in person, not by e-mail. Everyone likes to know when a job has been done well. That's when you can also give added responsibilities. By delegating, you save yourself time and build a team.

## Label your discard files

"When in doubt, throw it out." Self-proclaimed domestic engineering specialist Beatrice Ellwood used that simple rhyme to deal with clutter. With five children, there was a lot of clutter.

Similarly with e-mail, there are some files that you know you'll be deleting eventually. Label those to make them easier to find and delete. This tip also works well for word processing files.

Consider the situation where you're working on a current document called Budget Proposal. You make a number of revisions. Then you cut out a major section that's superfluous. Oops. You realize you wanted that section after all. What to do? Save the document and call it, say, Budget Proposal Revised. Then go back to the original Budget Proposal document, open it, and find the section you deleted. Cut it out, so that you can paste it into your revised document. Now if you really still want to keep the original document (whatever for, one might ask), you can save it. After you do, give it a new name, like 1Budget Proposal.

A month from now, go through your files for a regular purging. Sort them by file name. All of the documents with a "1" in front of them will appear at the beginning of the list. This is your indication that these files can definitely be erased.

You can do the same for e-mails you want to save. If you can't rename them, use your flag function to identify those you want to delete. Or move them to a file folder called "Delete" or "Temporary." Sort and purge. Live long and prosper.

## Break the last response chain

Stop playing tag. This is the elaborate correspondence game that has a simple objective – never be the last person to receive something. The game play is simple. Every time you receive something, you have to send something back. It's an absurd game of bureaucracy that contributes to e-mail glut.

An example will explain this game. Imagine two fictitious companies, Worldwide Office Supplies and Global Recruiting Incorporated. Global asks Worldwide for information on desks. Worldwide thanks Global and sends the information. Global sends confirmation that the information has been received, and promises to keep Worldwide posted. Worldwide asks if Global has made a decision and Global responds with a purchase order. Worldwide thanks Global for the order and indicates a delivery date. Global receives the desks and sends delivery confirmation, to which Worldwide responds with an invoice. Global asks for information to fill out a supplier form and Worldwide sends it. Global sends a check. Worldwide thanks Global for the check and hopes they can do business again. Global thanks Worldwide for the letter, and Worldwide sends a Christmas card. Global asks if any new vice presidents are needed, and Worldwide requests...(you guessed it), more information. The whole cycle starts again, with the parties changing places.

You don't always have to acknowledge an acknowledgement of a note thanking you for a thank-you card. Cut the glut.

## Set up a filing system

Your in-box is not a storage bin. Whenever your messages take up so much room that you have to scroll through them, it's time to set up additional file folders. Create folders to deal with:

- projects
- employees
- your manager
- training material
- interesting trivia

You can also create a place for "pending to-dos." These are the items you need to follow up next week. Or make a file called "Upcoming Events" for announcements about meetings that you need to attend. If you are selling, "Pending Business" will take care of inquiries from prospects that are still in the works. "Work in Progress" is for projects that are on the go right now. Once this gets too large, subdivide it for each project.

Are you a volunteer member of an association? Create a separate file for matters that pertain to the group's activities. If you want to save references, endorsements, or congratulatory notes, keep them in a separate file. For those times when customers feel they've received just a little less than your best, create a "Complaints" file.

James runs a business that sells products through the Internet. He receives orders through his web site. When he does, he sends out the product along with an invoice. (He's not yet ready for automated payments.) Each time he sends an invoice, the e-mail order goes into an "Unpaid Orders" file until the invoice is actually paid. This way, he can quickly send out reminder notices to everyone in that group, if needed. Pay on time, or you'll hear from James.

## Set expiry dates

"I just might possibly maybe need this someday, but I'm not sure." Does this sound like a familiar refrain? If so, you've probably got gigabytes of old messages congesting your system, your hard drive, or your e-mail server.

First, sort your e-mail and move your current messages out of your incoming mail folder, as described above. This way, the newer mail is not only easier to find but quicker to load (which is especially true when dialing in from a remote location on a slow connection). Delete old, duplicated or replied messages to make room for new incoming mail.

If you can't decide what old stuff to throw out, then set an expiry date. Ask yourself, at what point in the future will you no longer need to refer to current e-mail? A month from now is too short a time, while a year is probably more than enough time. When has anyone ever asked you to check your e-mail about something that happened a year ago? Set a rule for yourself. For example, on January 1st of each year, throw away everything from two years ago. Setting an expiry date works for e-mail, just as it works for clutter around your house or office.

# STOP SENDING SO MUCH E-MAIL

## Stop copying people

You keep getting stuff you don't need to be copied on. So what makes the stuff you cc to everyone any different? Younger readers may not know that cc stands for "carbon copy." Decades ago, the embossed keys on a standard typewriter struck against a ribbon of type, which created an inked impression on a sheet of paper. To make a second copy, you placed a sheet of carbon paper between two sheets of white bond. The carbon paper acted like a second printer ribbon, creating a duller version of the original. The recipient of the letter received the original while you kept the carbon copy. The more copies you made, the fainter they got. You could only copy as many people as you could make copies for – about a handful.

E-mail now allows you to copy the world. It's easier, too. No smudgy carbon paper and hard-to-read ink. No wasted time messing with the photocopier, stuffing copies into the internal mail, and waiting for the mail clerk to distribute them. Now, because people can send out lots of copies easily, they do. They're operating in "cover your butt" mode. If everyone knows what you're doing, no one can reprimand you. But what kind of way to work is this? Do you need to let your boss know every minuscule detail about what you're doing? No. Bosses are interested in results, not all the correspondence it took to get you there.

People say, "I need to be copied on stuff to stay in the loop." In fact, they're out of the loop because of all the time they're spending going through their e-mail in-basket.

So stop using the cc function or severely limit its use. This is drastic. It's "outside the box" thinking. But innovative thinking is necessary because in-boxes are overflowing. Allow employees to copy others if necessary, but they must send separate letters to each recipient, by cutting and pasting the contents as they go. This would slow down the sender and make him or her think twice about sending out additional copies. Also, in the process of cutting and pasting, the sender would add a personalized note to each new recipient to make comprehension easier. Drastic times call for drastic measures.

## Use bcc for broadcasting

All right, if you absolutely must send copies to people, use the bcc button, which stands for "blind carbon copy." Perhaps you want someone to receive a copy, but for whatever reason, don't want others to know this. In the past, you could send people their own copies without including their names on the cc list at the bottom of a printed letter. They would receive their "blind" copies, which was great for all sorts of corporate politics and intrigue.

The bcc function has now been incorporated into e-mail. If you have a group of people that really need to know what's going on but don't need to know each other, don't use the "to" line on your e-mail system. If you do, everyone will know who received a copy. The same thing happens when you use the cc function. Everyone can see the name of everyone else who received a copy. When you send broadcast announcements to different organizations this way, people get angry. They worry about other recipients picking up their addresses and creating new mailing lists.

By using the bcc function instead, no one will know who else received a copy. This is useful for broadcasting invitations to events or meetings. Or you can use it to send announcements about your business. Just remember the two cardinal rules of e-mail marketing: 1) Give people useful information that they can use. 2) Don't overwhelm people with messages.

What's too often? Once every four to six months keeps you in touch, but once a month is too soon. No one who's selling products or services needs to be in touch that much.

## Don't use the "Reply to All" button

It's bad enough that people use the cc function to send notes all over the place. Don't compound the problem by writing a response and hitting the "Reply to All" button. After all, when you copy 20 people, you're sending out 20 e-mails, and contributing to the glut. "But everyone needs to know," you might say. Do they really need to know?

One of the justifications for the "Reply to All" button is when you're feeling wronged. You want to set the record straight. When everyone knows you've been accused of not meeting your obligations, you feel the need to tell your side of the story. You don't need to. Mature, responsible people will know better than to fall for false accusations. You only raise suspicions when you respond with a vigorous defense to a weak indictment. Then things get messy when the originator of all this intrigue responds with a response to your response, which continues an endless cycle.

For those recipients who skipped the first round of messages, your response will be confusing. If they really want to know what happened, they'll let you know. And if you have nothing to be afraid of, let your actions speak louder than your words. Do your job, live up to your commitments, and stick with your point of view. Petty defenses make you look petty.

## Avoid spreading hoaxes

Scams, jokers, criminals, and fly-by-nighters love the Internet. Some of these people perpetrate seemingly harmless hoaxes, while others steal money. All of them steal time. When you send their messages to others, you're contributing to the glut. Be aware of what to look for and avoid forwarding hoaxes. Here's the cardinal rule: anytime you receive something that says, "Please send this to everyone you know!" you shouldn't.

One recent e-mail suggested that "the US Postal Service will be attempting to bill e-mail users alternative postage fees. Bill 602P will permit the Federal Government to charge a 5-cent surcharge on every e-mail delivered, by billing Internet service providers at source." Activate your critical-thinking mode and engage in a little detective work if you're at all suspicious. For instance, this hoax mentions an editorial in a newspaper called the *Washingtonian*. There's a magazine called that, but no paper. A member of congress is quoted who does not exist, and there's no mention of how the charges would be collected. Watch out for unsubstantiated claims or sources: "A friend told me that her cousin worked with someone who...."

Hoaxes are also obvious by their lack of date. You'll frequently receive requests to help locate lost children or to support a child who has cancer, but there is no date given. Here are some of the categories to watch out for:

- Giveaways – Large reputable organizations have money or products to give away if you simply forward e-mails.
- Requests to help – You'll be asked to send sympathy letters or to test a tracking system.
- Traditional chain letters – These threaten you with bad luck if you don't send them on, or promise you good luck if you do. There always seems to be some guy who wins a big lottery in Venezuela after passing on the letter.

- Pyramid schemes – You buy "reports" and sell them to others who sell them in turn, paying you along the way. Most are illegal.
- Urban myths – Fantastic stories sound as if they could have happened but are, in fact, just tall tales with infinite variations. One month a television star is featured in a story. The next time you read it, the star has morphed into a rock musician.
- Threat chains – Some chain letters appeal to your good nature to forward messages. These ones threaten that something bad will happen to your computer if you don't.
- Earn money at home – These schemes are legal but rip-offs. You buy supplies from a company and complete work to exacting specifications. When you can't produce to the extreme quality levels, you aren't paid for your work.

## Minimize autoresponders

"I'll be away on holidays until next week. In the meantime, I'm contributing to the e-mail glut." You won't ever receive a message with a second sentence like that, but you might as well. It's from an autoresponder, a feature that automatically sends out a response from you every time an e-mail is received. The idea is that if you are away, your e-mail can respond to people, even though you're not there. This is a seemingly good idea.

Unfortunately, this can end up creating a mail storm. Imagine a situation where an on-line investment discussion group automatically sends each new posting to everyone on its list. People want to keep abreast, so they receive all of the postings. One day Sarah Kramer, a list participant, sets up an autoresponder to notify everyone that she'll be away. Then, one of the regular postings from the investing group hits Sarah's in-box. Her autoresponder sends back her vacation note to the group. That message in turn gets sent to all of the participants, including another note back to her autoresponder, which responds again. Suddenly everyone on the list begins receiving all of this junk. So they send notes to the mailing list to tell the administrator to fix the problem or indicate that they would like to unsubscribe. These too get sent to Sarah, and the problem multiplies. This is not a pretty scene.

Autoresponders contribute to glut because they send an e-mail for every one they receive. If you can't afford an assistant to go through your mail daily, it's certainly worth paying someone do it while you're on vacation. After all, what fun is it to come back refreshed from a relaxing trip, only to discover 300 e-mails?

Perhaps a good use of autoresponders is in sending back particular information. For instance, if you have a web site, you can offer to send people useful information, articles, or tips if they send a request to a particular address. Also, use them for frequently requested information such as brochures, price lists, directions, etc. Set up an e-mail at your web site, such as info@mycompany.com, as a separate address from your own.

## Ignore the jokes and trivia

Three guys walk into a bar. The bartender has heard this joke before. So he kicks them out and tells them to stop cluttering up his e-mail in-box.

Do you save all those dumb jokes that people send you? What for? Are you really going to spend an afternoon going through them a second time? If you really want a good laugh, there are plenty of humor web sites to visit.

Whatever you do with jokes, don't send them on. You don't want to get a reputation as someone who needlessly contributes to e-mail glut. Save your jokes for lunch or after-hours at the bar.

Why are there so many jokes circulating? The Internet is touted as a way of fostering greater community. But because people now work in isolation, they feel less connected. Sending jokes and trivia is their way of staying in touch. Without a water cooler to gather around or a cafeteria to eat lunch in, employees seek out ways to form bonds and associations. So they send jokes through the Internet. The need for affiliation is a powerful force.

Look for ways to recapture your sense of community. Plan department get-togethers. Sponsor a casual pizza lunch every couple of months. Make your staff meetings meaningful. Create a newsletter to inform employees about work matters as well as personal accomplishments. They're worth it.

## Beware of contests

"CONGRATULATIONS! You have been selected as a finalist in the XXYZ Travel Giveaway. Prizes are accommodations for two nights at any of the following locations: Fort Lauderdale, Bahamas, Branson, Las Vegas, Williamsburg, Orlando." This is the beginning of an actual message. These are all fine places to visit, but they're not exactly Paris, Rome, or London. The contest provides two nights accommodation, which sounds swell. But you have to get there. You have to pay for your meals. You have to rent a car. You have to pay for admission to attractions. If you have children, you have to pay for a baby-sitter back home. And on and on. Unlike Internet hoaxes or illegal scams, many of these offers originate from legitimate companies. However, their free offer is often just a low-cost way for them to meet you so they can sell you time-sharing vacations.

There are some contests that are legitimate. For instance, packaged goods manufacturers run contests to create consumer awareness for their brand and to encourage retailers to put up big displays in their stores. If you're interested, by all means apply, but be aware that everything has a price, including your name and address. For the most part, the manufacturers aren't interested in who you are. But they could sell a list with your name on it. Leave off your e-mail address. If you win, they'll find a way to reach you through your phone number.

## Return messages slowly

What's the hurry? Slow down. Wait to respond. If you receive an e-mail message that's not urgent, avoid the temptation to reply to it right away. Wait. Then wait some more. This advice flies in the face of everything you've learned about instant communication. After all, what's the point of using an almost instantaneous medium if you're going to wait? The reality is that many people are driven by an irrational need for speed. They feel important because they are so much in demand that others want instant answers from them. They believe their status and their work performance are determined by an ability to respond quickly.

This is certainly true for some jobs. For instance, with doctors, real estate agents, and subway maintenance workers, quick action is required. But for many jobs, people have created an artificial sense of urgency. With traditional mail, things used to be expected in a couple of days. Then couriers promised next day delivery. Fax machines shortened expectations to a few hours. E-mail has condensed time frames to an hour or less. Now with instant messaging, people expect instant responses. The trouble is, you can't get any faster than instant. There's nowhere to go. So when someone sends you a message, he or she gets upset. "It's been 30 seconds now and I haven't heard back! What's going on?"

You can't change expectations. If someone wants a quick response, you need to get back to him or her quickly, however they define a quick response. But you don't need to encourage it. When you rush to respond, you're training people to raise their expectations. So slow down. When it isn't necessary, take your time to respond. You'll be surprised that most people will find this acceptable. Send that e-mail response later, on your schedule, not someone else's. Most e-mails can wait.

## Create groups

The little black book has changed into a little black screen. Learn how to use an electronic address book to store e-mail addresses, automatically insert them into a new message, and maintain groups of contacts.

Earlier advice discouraged using the cc and bcc functions too often. However, there are occasions when using them can improve your productivity. If you have a master list of addresses, you can create subgroups of your addresses. Send yourself an e-mail and bcc everyone in the subgroup when you need to broadcast. For instance, a sales manager might want to send an e-mail to all of the sales team announcing a price change. Within this broader group, only the key account managers can be e-mailed to inform them of a special promotional program available to national accounts. Not everyone needs to see this.

If you're announcing a meeting that everyone has to attend, using the bcc button is appropriate. For personal matters, you can create an invitation list for your next party. Welcome your in-laws to the digital age.

## Avoid the free stuff

In the commercial world, nothing is ever free. Ask yourself, why is someone offering me this no cost, risk free, lifetime-lasting proposal? What's in it for them? The answer is plenty.

While they may not want you to pay now, the "free" enticement often lasts for a "limited time only." You'll have to pay later. Or, perhaps the offer is free, but you'll need to make a purchase later on. Consider cellular phones. You can get a free phone, but you'll need to pay for airtime. Similarly, you can get free Internet access, but you'll have to put up with a lot of advertising.

With television, conventional network programming is free, but networks are selling audiences to advertisers. Perhaps you don't mind the occasional interruption, but remember that 25% of conventional television is advertising – a huge demand on your time. The Internet hasn't quite figured out its business models yet, but be careful of free services disguised to show you ads. You'll be besieged by web pages of no interest that pop up when you least expect. Many of these enticements come over e-mail. E-mail systems themselves are often offered at no cost, but there is always a cost. Nothing is really free and good things are worth paying for.

## Be diplomatic in making requests

Your project is late and those guys are to blame. It's always "them," isn't it? When you're working with other departments, there are times when they let you down. E-mails fly back and forth with little being accomplished. How do you avoid losing your patience when others are being inefficient or evasive? Not losing patience is a common concern. Based on Pace Productivity research, employees rate dealing with other departments' inefficiency as their fifth most common productivity problem (after paperwork, customer requests, phone interruptions, and computer problems).

In dealing with others, begin with the assumption that they are as competent as you are. Everyone is doing his or her best, and everyone is busy. Remember that ultimately you're all on the same team. Your positive attitude will get better results than antagonism. Treat them as you would like to be treated.

Make your requests in the same way you would delegate to a subordinate. 1) Clarify the task to be done and the standards to be met. 2) Establish a timetable. 3) Ask if there is anything else the person needs to begin. 4) Confirm others' commitment.

Despite your best intentions, someone will occasionally let you down. When this occurs, you may have a tendency to react with one of two opposite emotions – aggression or passivity. Aggression is fighting back, yelling, name-calling, threatening to inform a higher authority, becoming impatient, and being forceful. This kind of reaction is going to get you nowhere. Reacting aggressively is bad enough in person. Doing so through e-mail is almost certain to make you look foolish. Passivity is giving in, ignoring an issue, procrastinating, or apologizing. When an issue becomes a crisis, avoid using e-mail. Make your request in person or over the phone. Be assertive and polite. Use the person's name, and say "please" and "thank-you." Ask for help instead of telling someone what to do.

---

## Be assertive

When someone has really messed up, avoid an e-mail response. Otherwise, you'll sound demanding. Use the phone or a meeting and be straightforward with your request: "Our department needs this delivered to us by tomorrow." Adding an explanation helps to validate the request. Then ask if they need anything else, or if you can do anything to help the process. Clarify the agreement you made.

If the person objects, repeat the request by stating it slightly differently each time. "Jillian, I'd like to get a copy of that report by tomorrow." She answers that she's too busy. "I can understand how you've got a big workload. (Avoid the dreaded "but") I do need the report finished by tomorrow, so can we find a way to complete it somehow?"

Ask "Would it be helpful if I…." Sometimes people can do a better job if you can help them first. Your offer also displays genuine empathy.

Use the phrase, "What would have to happen...." For instance, "I understand most of the staff have left for the day. What would have to happen for this to be finished by tomorrow morning?" People will stumble and say that it's not possible. Agree with them, then assertively repeat the phrase. "What *would* have to happen…?" Sometimes the person might suggest a solution that you can help achieve: "Well I'd have to send it over in a taxi and we're not allowed to do that." Maybe they can't authorize a taxi, but you can.

Don't appeal to a higher authority, but appeal to someone's interests. If you say, "I need this done, and I can get my boss to authorize you to speed things up if I have to," you'll be less successful than if you show an interest in how their child is doing at soccer.

Always make the assumption that people are genuinely doing their best. They're not lazy or incompetent. They simply need your help, guidance, or clarification in moving your project to its proper priority.

Ask them what the holdups are and set up a meeting to outline your concerns. The other department might identify blocks that can be easily removed. You can get the help you need by helping others.

## Don't pass on virus warnings

Everyone loves to be helpful and the advent of e-mail has made it much easier for so many people to feel as if they're doing some good. If only that were true. In reality, the proliferation of false virus warnings, chain letters, and money-making schemes jams up the Internet and wastes time. No one can be quite sure how hoaxes get started, nor why someone would start them, but there are many hoaxes. The hook in the subject line draws you in. "Warning – Dangerous New Virus!" Then comes the actual threat. "This virus will destroy your hard drive and cause your eyeballs to pop out at the same time." The message will have all sorts of technical-sounding mumbo jumbo that seems to make sense. There may be references to credible-sounding sources such as IBM and Microsoft. Since you can never be quite sure, you trust what the warning says. You figure you'd rather be safe than sorry.

When in doubt, don't panic. The warnings can be hoaxes. In a large organization, contact your system administrator before you pass on warnings. If you run your own business, go to legitimate anti-virus software web sites. Most have sections that list hoaxes.

Here's the cardinal rule: whenever someone sends you an e-mail and implores you to send it to everyone you know, don't.

One way to avoid viruses is by not opening e-mail attachments. If you receive an attachment with an .exe extension, treat it as highly suspicious because that's an executable program that can cause damage. Viruses can hide in innocuous document files as well, and "read" your address book to send themselves out to everyone in it. As much as possible, know what people are sending you. Do the same for others by writing cover notes with descriptions of your attachments.

## Institute a "No E-Mail Day"

A few years back, no executive at a large corporation would have dreamed of wearing casual pants to work on a Friday. Casual dress days began as a way to raise money for local charities. Everyone chipped in for the privilege of dressing down. The movement caught on and the casual, youthful attire of the software industry encouraged it. Everyone wanted to do business with the young people who were "pulling all-nighters" at their keyboards. The trend could swing back, but clearly there is more room for casual styles than a decade ago.

It's time to create a similar new movement with a "No E-Mail Day." Get agreement from your team in advance and proclaim an edict that on a certain day, no e-mail will be sent. Of course, you're going to have to announce this. It would be nice if it wasn't through e-mail – this obviously defeats the point!

Julie, a government acquaintance remarked, "That idea won't work. Business is done by e-mail. You might as well declare a day off!" In fact, the idea is deliberately radical. It's an "outside the box" approach that's meant to break patterns. Also, a "No E-Mail Day" isn't just about asking people to substitute other ways of being in touch. More than that, this approach gives people permission to take a break from e-mail so they can work on other high-priority projects. There's never enough time for the high-priority "A" activities: planning, creating, managing, coaching, designing, and analyzing. People say they would do more of these if they had the time, yet they're bogged down by all the "B" activities. Carve out time to do the important stuff by taking a break from e-mail now and then. You'll be surprised at what you can get done.

## Don't attach large files

The glut of e-mail is not just the volume of e-mail you receive but the amount of file space it takes up. Don't send large files without getting permission from your recipient first. People receiving this stuff become resentful of how long these files take to download. This is particularly true for files that include a lot of graphics. (Those vacation photos can jam up a server very quickly.) Here's an example from a consultant of what not to send:

> In our conversations with clients, it is clear that everyone is struggling with a host of people concerns resulting from current economic conditions. At XXYZ Company, we have done a great deal of thinking and talking with clients about these people management issues over the last several months and have prepared the attached document to share our perspectives. I trust you will find these concise materials thoughtful and would be delighted to talk with you further about how these issues might be manifesting in your business. Feel free to give me a call at....

This e-mail breaks many rules. First, there is no personalization, as in "Dear Mark." The attached document is also huge at 219 kilobytes and is hardly "concise." The message is six pages and over 3,000 words long. The document uses 10-point type, which is very small to read. Consequently, the lines are too long, ranging up to 25 words. The document also goes from a single column to two columns, which is graphically awkward, and includes a chart containing 12 cryptic boxes, three of which are filled in. The chart might make sense when explained, but it's not intuitively obvious from a quick glance. Don't make these kinds of mistakes.

Many office workers are now inundated with warnings from their IT departments or system administrators. Their files are taking up too much space and there's no more room for new e-mail. So they have to delete old files now. Don't be part of the problem.

## Sleep on it

Sending emotional e-mails is a no-no. Don't be the instigator of angry e-mails, or those that lay blame. Don't try to shun responsibility by outlining a long series of confusing steps that occurred. ("On Monday, after visiting you, I forwarded your comments to Dick who indicated that he would not be able to attend the meeting even though he had previously committed to do so after I had personally asked him at your request...blah, blah, blah.")

Although you may not be the sender, chances are, at some point, you'll receive an e-mail that shuns diplomacy and embraces belligerence. When someone puts you in an awkward position or makes you look less than responsible, your first instinct might be to respond instantly and set the record straight. You could defend yourself or redirect the blame elsewhere but this is asking for trouble. Someone else (who hasn't read this book) might forward your response all over the organization. You'll end up looking petty, foolish, and irresponsible. Or there may be a counter response. If someone was originally "out to get you," chances are they'll keep trying with more evidence and accusations. E-mails will then ricochet back and forth, like smacked ping-pong balls, which will just make things worse.

You have a few alternatives. One is to let the matter cool down a bit. Sleep on it to give yourself the perspective of time. In the meantime, you could send an e-mail that says, "I received your e-mail about the errors in the monthly report. I'll get back to you with a response tomorrow morning."

Better than that, try a personal visit. People seem much more civilized in face to face conversations than when they're sending e-mails.

Your third response is humility. Accept responsibility without laying blame. Apologize if necessary, and indicate how you are going to rectify the problem or make amends. No one can argue with that. As Mark Twain said, "Good breeding consists in concealing how much we think of ourselves and how little we think of the other person."

## Stop sending newsletters

Do your receive those saccharine Christmas letters with their excruciating details of the year's minutiae? "Jamie's happy that his new job is working out while Sarah has taken up Spanish lessons, blah, blah...." You read through them not with the excitement of anticipation but with the drudgery of resentment. Every minor event is accorded the importance of a world leaders' summit. Come to think of it, those are pretty boring, too.

An earlier chapter encouraged you to discontinue your e-mail newsletter subscriptions. You can set an example and cut the glut of e-mail by discontinuing the ones you write as well. People aren't interested in what you've got to report unless it makes a difference to their lives.

Consultants marketing their services send regular weekly e-mail newsletters to keep them in touch with a broad audience: customers, prospects, media, and friends. However, with the glut of e-mail out there, knowing how to stand out is difficult. Not only that, but people who receive your regular communications say to themselves, "Here's another newsletter from Jones. Maybe I'll get to it later." Or, "I might as well delete this. It's just the usual drivel." This is not the kind of reaction you want. What you hope for is someone who thinks, "Hey look, there's something from Smith. Haven't heard from him for a while. I wonder what interesting insights he's got for me this time?" You can create that reaction by reducing the frequency of your updates. Weekly or biweekly newsletters are too often. Even monthly ones can be excessive, depending on the kind of business you're in. If you're selling services and you're in touch with prospects two to three times per year via e-mail, that's probably sufficient.

When you write, keep the commercial content to a minimum. The best way to build credibility is to give people information they can use. Provide tips, updates, research, or insights. Avoid telling people how great your products or services are; they'll find out when they're ready.

# WRITE PROFESSIONALLY

## Don't intersperse your comments

Charlie and his wife Samantha give great parties. They recently sent out invitations to their annual tacky outfit ball. ("Bring out the bridesmaids' horrors....") Most invitations went by traditional mail, but since they didn't have everyone's address, they reluctantly sent a few by e-mail. Samantha included a few other points in an invitation to her friend Bernard – movies to see, a couple of political comments, and a query about his vacation. He responded a couple of days later. Sadly, Samantha announced to her husband that Bernard wouldn't be attending the party. Apparently he was holding a party of his own on the same night. Only on further examination did Charlie discover (to his wife's slight embarrassment) that Bernard had interspersed his comments in Samantha's original e-mail. Buried in the middle of his message was Samantha's message. Small arrows appeared in front of her comments, but with all the inserts, the note was difficult to read.

Interspersing responses in the original e-mail is a lazy way to respond. When an e-mail has a series of numbered questions, interspersing comments would make sense. But most people don't send e-mails that way. They make points throughout their paragraphs and throw in questions where appropriate, so responding with inserts makes for a tough read.

Instead, write a proper, full response. Typing, "Regarding your question about pricing..." takes longer but makes reading the response much easier.

## Check for spelling errors

"It's just e-mail. No one minds a few spelling errors." In fact, they do. There's a convention that since e-mail is a relatively casual medium, small errors are acceptable as long as the essence of the message is clear. However, errors are not acceptable because they slow down the reader's comprehension and take away from your professional reputation. And if your note is forwarded to someone else, the effect is compounded.

When you receive something sloppily written, what do you think of the writer? You probably think a little less of him or her than you did previously. It's almost like discovering someone you respect has a terrible case of bad breath or ugly "toe jam."

"Bob's a terrific mentor. He's kind, caring, knowledgeable."

"Yeah but don't get too close to him. He always smells kind of funny."

"That's nothing! Ever get an e-mail from him? The guy doesn't know how to spell!"

Check the spelling of your e-mail before sending it. Use an automatic spell checker every time. Others may say that spelling errors are acceptable, but why settle for being acceptable? Aim for excellence and create an image that is outstanding.

## Re-read your e-mail before sending it

Writing quickly results in awkward grammar, so check what you've written by re-reading your e-mail after you've composed it. Spell checkers will catch obvious errors, but not all of them. Here are a few common rules to remember:

- Be sure that subjects agree with verbs and with each other. For instance, indefinite pronouns are singular: "Everyone in the office is working on his or her (not "their") budget." "The programs that I installed in the computer appear (not "appears") to be damaged." "A printer and modem are (not "is") required."
- Be careful with apostrophes. "It's not until November when my oak tree sheds its leaves." (The first is a contraction; the second is a possessive.)
- Avoid redundancies. "The reason (not "reason why") our sales fell short stems (not "stems mainly") from lack of customer awareness." (Not "existing customer.")
- Adjectives modify nouns. Adverbs modify verbs. "The schedule worked out perfectly (not "perfect") for everyone." "His speech went over really well." (Not "real well.")
- Use commas everywhere in a list. "The budget includes provisions for emergencies, prolonged absences, and bad weather." (Most experts advise using the last comma to avoid ambiguity.)

- Do not split infinitives needlessly. "If possible, attendees should try to arrive on time." (Not "attendees should try to, if possible, arrive on time.")
- Use "that" and "which" with caution. Essential, limiting information uses "that" and no commas; nonessential, descriptive information uses "which," with commas. The latter functions as if "by the way" were inserted after it. For instance, "Please be on time for the classes that interest you. If you have to quit, write a note, which must be typed, to explain your reasons."
- Use commas to help the reader. "When he finished his lunch, he went for a walk, knowing that he would be late."
- When a subject or object is part of a compound structure, test for the right word by stripping away all of the compound word group except the pronoun in question. "Megan went with her staff and me to the meeting." (Megan went with "me," not "I.")

Finally, remember Jonathan Swift's advice on writing:

> Blot out, correct, insert, refine,
> Enlarge, diminish, interline;
> Be mindful, when invention fails,
> To scratch your head, and bite your nails.

## Write attention-getting subject lines

This tip will get you immediate results. Now, there's an attention-getting sentence. Busy people are attracted to e-mails with captivating subject lines. Consider the techniques spammers use. These techniques are annoying, but they work.

- Use short power words such as free, now, instant, improve, and fast.
- Talk to your audience. Would you respond to "Attend a short planning meeting today from 2-3 p.m." or "Meeting announcement"? Would you be more inclined to answer "Information needed" or "Need your expertise on pricing"?
- Flatter people. "Thanks for the great party" is better than "RE: RE: RE: Party Invitation," which results from a series of e-mails sent back and forth.
- Create a call to action. Someone looking to buy training seminars will get a faster response with "Please contact me" instead of "Workshop."
- Make your subject lines personal, but don't be sloppy. Subject lines that say "Hey" or "Hello" or "Hi" are lazy. On the other hand, subject lines that say "I saw this and thought of you" appeal to the reader directly. Who could resist that kind of subject line? Some spammers get a little presumptuous with "The information you requested" when you did no such thing. Still, it grabs your attention. Just be sure to check the contents when you receive one of these. An enticing sounding subject

line ("I love you") could be a disguise for an attachment with a virus.

## Avoid long signature lines

The signature line appears as a sign-off at the bottom of each e-mail you send and is like a letterhead, except that it appears at the bottom rather than at the top. Once you set up the signature line, it appears automatically on the e-mails you send. The signature line is useful in newsgroups because people can see your e-mail address and quickly get back to you personally. Or, if you include a web site address, they can click on it.

You can set up your signature line to say whatever you like, and include links, too, but keep it short. Including a slogan for your business on a single line is reasonable. What's not reasonable is a slogan, plus a list of major areas of specialty, alternate phone numbers, etc. And don't junk it up with lines of asterisks, dashes or other unnecessary characters. E-mail text is sent in plain text. That means you can't use much to dress up your letters, so don't try.

The latest goofy signature lines probably began in the legal profession and have rapidly spread. They include all kinds of legal-sounding mumbo jumbo about how this e-mail contains privileged information. Not only that, but if you weren't supposed to get it, then you should let the sender know. This is all a bit silly. Your e-mail shouldn't contain sensitive information to begin with. The chances of other individuals receiving it in error are quite small. Even if it does reach someone inadvertently, most people will react by destroying it in frustration, not copying it gleefully.

## Use active language

Write in the active mode. Or, to put it differently, it is considered important that e-mail correspondence is to be written not without a degree of positive emphasis. Why is it so hard for people to say "you"? It all started with the airline business: "Passengers are requested to fasten their seatbelts." "Luggage is to be stowed in the overhead bins or under the seat." The passive mode is used by people to sound corporate and official. Oops. It's spreading. Let's try that again. Corporations try to sound official by using the passive mode.

In the active voice, the subject of the sentence does the action; in the passive, the subject receives the action. Both are correct, but the active voice is more effective because it is simpler and more direct. Passive language is impersonal and indirect. Don't hide behind passivity. Be clear about the verbs you use. Be active, not passive.

## Don't put messages in subject lines

The subject line is not the message, but is a way to summarize your note. The subject line draws the reader's attention, and encourages him or her to read on. Here's how not to do it, with an actual subject line as it appeared in a note to a nonprofit group called the Inventors' Alliance:

> Subscribe. Please send me Inven…

That was it. There was no note attached in the e-mail, just the headline. Only by clicking on the headline does the full message appear:

> Subscribe. Please send me Inventors' meeting agendas for Toronto.

The first problem is that the message is buried in the subject line. This is lazy for the writer and troublesome for the reader. The subject line is too long.

Another problem with this particular e-mail is that the writer did not indicate an e-mail address on the "from" line. That means you have to click on the message properties and look up where the message came from, then recopy it to an address book. This is a time-consuming process. The way to short-circuit this is to look for a feature in your e-mail menu that allows you to "Add Sender to Address Book." When you're making a request through e-mail, make it easy for the reader to take the action you want.

## Be concise

Be simple. Get to the point. Use short sentences. Less is more.

Blaise Pascal confessed that "I have made this letter longer than usual, because I lack the time to make it short."

## Kill the acronyms

Acronyms and abbreviations are annoying. In e-mail correspondence, you'll discover such gems as IMHO (In My Humble Opinion) FWIW (For What It's Worth), LOL (Laughing Out Loud) and OMG (Oh My God). First, these are trite expressions. Professional writing deserves to be as elegant as possible. Elegance means clear and understandable, not necessarily fancy. Excess idioms simply clutter up what would otherwise be good writing.

More importantly, IMHO, these expressions slow the reader down. Check out that last sentence. To understand it, you have to repeat the phrase in your mind to put it in context. That's a lot of work to ask of the reader. Make it easy. There are some acronyms such as IBM, NBC, NASA and NATO that have entered the public consciousness. They are acceptable. Others are not so clear. When you mention B.C., is that a province of Canada, or a period of time that ended just about 2,000 years ago?

Abbreviations are needed when there is no room to write details. Highway signs, for instance, have to communicate a lot with little. But if you don't need to abbreviate, then don't. Here's an actual classified ad from a government newsletter:

> For Sale: Mattress: nw, kg sz +2bx springs, stl pckgd, cost $1000, askng $375; bthtub enc, gls w/gold frame, $30; File Cabinet: lgl sz, 4-drwr, top-of-the-line, like nw, $75.

What confusion! The ads are free to employees, so it's not as if someone is paying by the letter and wants to save a few dollars. Check the word near the end, "nw." What's the point of leaving out a single letter? And is the bathtub "enclosed" in the package with the mattress? No wonder it needs two box springs!

## Write with your audience in mind

Who is your audience? When you send an e-mail, consider who will read it. Here are some questions to ask:

- Is the reader familiar with the subject? If not, you need to provide some background.
- What is the reader's disposition towards the subject at hand? Perhaps he or she is positively inclined and favorable towards your proposal. Or perhaps the reader has a bias that you know about. In that case, more convincing is needed. If someone is dead set against a project, you aren't likely to convince him or her through e-mail. You're better

off meeting in person, so you can engage in a dialogue and negotiate.

- Is your reader a decision-maker, an information gatherer or an influencer? Human resource managers are the people who gather information about training courses. The sales manager will recommend the courses once they find out about them. But the actual decision to attend might be up to the individual sales rep. If you're selling services, don't spend too much time corresponding with someone who is not a decision-maker. Nonetheless, respect those who act as screens and can help influence decision-makers.
- Do you have a relationship with your reader? If not, personal comments will seem overly familiar.
- Is your reader appreciated? You can be the person who brightens your reader's day by being thankful, providing positive feedback, or sending a note of congratulations.

## Choose your words wisely

Have you ever received an e-mail that sounds like this?

> As per our earlier discussion regarding the previously mentioned subject to which you inquired, we are respectfully submitting herewith a reply in response to your inquiry. We are pleased to be able to forward to you the relevant documentation which will have as an objective, the goal of communicating the salient points

> summarizing the items and/or service and/or benefit which you had requested and/or indicated an interest in. Blah, blah, blah.

This is what could be called "important talk." You can also hear it by eavesdropping on cellular phone conversations in airports. People want to sound important, so they speak in language that sounds big. In fact it's off-putting. Write simply and clearly. Impress people with clarity, not obscurity.

A second problem with words is using too much jargon. Talk to anyone involved with computers, and that's what you'll get. Have you ever noticed that people often talk about their computers the way they used to talk about their cars? The two begin to sound the same:

> I just bought a beauty. It's got fuel-injection RAM, antilock keyboard brakes, 400 gigabyte hard drive steering with an active matrix TFT display on the dash, an overhead cam cable modem, and high-speed CD burner. Runs like a charm.

Avoid jargon.

Another inappropriate style is casual writing. Imagine receiving an e-mail about an important project: "That guy's work is the pits. Let's give him the boot. See ya."

Avoid colloquialisms and flippancy. A rule of thumb is to imagine that whatever you write would be circulated to the entire company, including the president. What would you want him or her to read?

## Tell people what you want

Years ago at Procter & Gamble, brand managers learned the science of writing "the one-page document." The first rule was that every document had to start with the word "this" followed by a verb in the present tense. So documents would begin with "This recommends..." or "This updates..." or "This summarizes...." The style was occasionally lampooned for its excessive rigidity, but it was a simple and effective way of communicating what was wanted of the reader, and also helped the writer organize his or her thoughts.

You don't have to use a style as rigid as that, but you should make it clear to people why you are writing and what you want. Do you want them to provide information, complete a request, contact someone, or show up for a meeting? Be clear. Here are some examples:

- Could you please forward the upcoming dates for your seminar program?
- I'd like to get a refund for a defective product I recently purchased.
- You're invited to attend the next meeting of the Process Improvement committee on October 14 at 10:00 a.m.
- Could you please send me the phone number for Helen Downey?
- What time is the staff meeting tomorrow?

An earlier tip recommended the abolition of the cc function. If you must copy someone or forward notes, then give the recipient some context. Add a short note at the top explaining why you are copying someone. Think of your reader and tell him or her what you want.

Do not overwhelm the reader though. You're contributing to the glut of e-mail when you send out an e-mail, then a follow-up with additional information, then a follow-up to the follow-up with another detail. Think through what you need to say and get it right the first time. Otherwise, your recipient will ignore you.

Finally, never send reminders. If people have agreed to go to a meeting or complete a task, they are responsible for scheduling their time. Filling up their in-boxes with trivial and unnecessary reminders is not your duty. If they made a commitment, expect them to stick to it without your help.

## Do away with emoticons

What's an emoticon and why would you want to get rid of it? An emoticon is a symbol made up of characters on your keyboard. There are other names for those cute little symbols that people insert into messages as a novel way of expressing an emotion. The smiley was the first and most popular of these. It's usually placed at the end of a sentence or paragraph, like this. : ) Sideways, it looks like a face. It's often used as a sign-off, a shorthand way of saying "yours truly."

After the smiley came into usage, people started developing variations to show a shocked face, one that was smoking, someone screaming and so on. You need a glossary of sorts to know what they are. And that's a warning signal not to use them.

Anytime you need a glossary to decipher a cryptic symbol, you shouldn't use the symbol, as readers won't know what your symbol means. Teenagers send all sorts of text messages with elaborate coding systems. (Can't they just talk to each other?) That may be fun for them, but it's unprofessional and difficult to figure out if you're in the business world. So don't worry about having to learn your child's latest codes. The codes will probably be defunct within a year anyway.

## Update the subject line

It's March and you receive an e-mail about a meeting that you organized two months before in January. What happened? The subject line is old. The person who sent the note hit the respond button in response to a previous note that was a response to a note that was sent to you. The person didn't change the subject line, which is appropriate when the subject is the same. But when notes go back and forth numerous times, then get forwarded to others, the thread of the subject can change along the way, with new issues being brought up. When this happens, change the subject line. Make it easy for your reader to understand what the note is about.

## Be a detective

What's the fastest way to insult someone? Spell his or her name wrong. There are many other ways to show a lack of investigative skills. This first one shows a writer floundering in her own ineptitude:

> I looked on your web site for the e-mail address of the person in charge of on-line marketing for GetMoreDone.com. I wasn't able to determine who that person is. If I send an e-mail to this address, will it be forwarded to the appropriate person?
>
> -Heather

First, in a relatively small company, you could expect that the business owner is also the person "in charge of on-line marketing." Second, there is no benefit statement in this letter. Why would someone want to respond? If the letter promised more web site visitors, more sales, or more leads, it would be much more compelling.

Job seekers are also guilty of sloppy research. If you're going to send a resume, personalize the letter you send. Here is another example of someone who simply hasn't done her homework:

> Dear Sir/Madam,
>
> I am interested in submitting a resume to your company. Can you tell me to what address I should send it? Thanks for your time!
>
> -Lea

Both e-mail and snail mail addresses can usually be found on the company's web site, as well as the name of the president. Job seekers who don't do their research are not worth hiring, or, for that matter, are not even worth responding to.

In the following note, the reverse occurs. The writer forces the reader to do the detective work. Which Joannie is sending this? Is this her new address or her old one?

> Dear Friends and Family: Please note the e-mail address change. Joannie@xxyz.com

The Internet opens up new ways to learn about an organization. If you are selling to, buying from, or trying to get a job with a company, much of the information will be on the web site. But don't limit yourself to that. You can do your detective work by requesting a copy of an annual report. Call up the switchboard (if there is one) and ask for information. Or ask who would have the information. Make it easy for people to respond and make it worth their time: "I'm interested in buying one of your products and I wanted to find out...."

Look slightly farther and you'll discover plenty of sources of information: articles and job ads in the newspaper, the company's suppliers and retailers, trade shows, and consumer exhibitions. Companies that engage in competitive intelligence-gathering have even been known to count cars in the parking lot! You can learn a lot when you think outside the box. Emulate Sherlock Holmes.

---

## Stop shouting!!!

DON'T WRITE IN ALL CAPITAL LETTERS. Books aren't written in capital letters because capital letters are difficult to read. To create emphasis, use descriptive adjectives, or add an exclamation point if necessary. But definitely, positively, absolutely don't use redundant words (as in this sentence) and beware of using a series of exclamation points!!! This is amateurish writing since you appear to be shouting in desperation. The same goes for question marks. Do you really need more than one???

Another type of shouting is the use of hypertext to create "cool" backgrounds and special effects. Unfortunately, fancy designs won't make up for bad writing, and designing all those effects takes up extra time that you don't have. Keep it simple and stick to basic text. Yet another form of shouting is the use of "priority" tags that attach to e-mails you send. Derek, an account manager with a large consulting firm says,

> You never see "urgent" or "high-priority" tags from presidents. You only see them from people low down in the organization trying to make what they're doing look

important. People overuse them, and the tags lose their impact. I ignore stuff from those people.

The moral of the story? Don't use "priority" tags.

## Say "please" and "thank-you"

We need to bring back civility. Have you ever read a letter or e-mail that says, "Please remit your overdue payment without delay or you will face severe repercussions. Thank-you." This isn't polite. It's stern!

Inserting "please" and "thank-you" into your e-mail requests is a start. There are other ways of being grateful. Perhaps you need something urgently, and you're partly to blame for the lateness of the situation. Try something like, "Jim, I feel bad that I wasn't able to ask you earlier, but I wonder if you could possibly squeeze in a few minutes to send me the information I need for the budget. I'll owe you one. Thanks." All right, so it sounds a bit like groveling. Humility never hurt anyone.

Another way to show your gratitude is to explain why you are thankful: "Melanie, I just wanted to drop a note to tell you how much I appreciated the extra effort you put into that proposal. It really made a difference in the presentation, and we got the go-ahead to proceed. Thanks again." As Lady Mary Wortley Montagu said, "Civility costs nothing and buys everything."

# USE ALTERNATIVES TO E-MAIL

## Use the phone instead

Whatever happened to the phone? Don't send e-mails when a phone call would be more appropriate. This is especially true for personnel issues. Here is a useful rule: if you find yourself spending a lot of time writing an e-mail, then rewriting it, fine-tuning it, and removing the awkward parts, it's time for a phone call.

For instance, use the phone instead of trying to describe a complicated series of events: "On Tuesday, when I called you with my order, your service representative confirmed that the delivery would be made if I faxed in a confirmation before 5:00 p.m. At 4:30 p.m., your fax machine appeared to be busy, so I was not able to send the fax until 5:15 p.m. The following day, I e-mailed to inquire whether the late fax would be acceptable, to which…blah, blah, blah." This is just asking for trouble.

Or perhaps you have a complaint or an admonition. You're steaming mad and it's time to let someone know. If you're feeling emotional about something, don't use e-mail. It's very difficult to convey genuine emotion through writing. Even positive praise works better when it's delivered in person. Use the phone when you are:

- mad at someone for letting you down
- concerned about an employee's recent performance or lack of it

- praising someone
- negotiating details
- making an important announcement
- offering a job
- firing an employee
- cutting back on bonuses

For any of these situations, a conversation in person works best of all. The higher quality the medium, the better the results.

Even sarcasm and humor are difficult to convey via e-mail. Sarcasm usually involves a particular tone of voice that telegraphs, "I'm not actually being too serious about this." There's no tone in e-mail, so your message may make sense to you, but someone doing a quick read might not understand your meaning. The same goes for humor. Writing humor is difficult to do. Leave it to the professionals.

## Stop multi-tasking

"Hey everybody, look at me! I can talk on the phone, respond to my e-mail, eat lunch, and lift weights at the same time. All while I'm stuck in traffic!" People who feel busy feel productive. But being productive is not just about doing a lot of things; it's about doing the right things. And being productive is certainly not about doing many things at once. Those who simultaneously attempt multiple tasks display what they think is an extraordinary skill. They'll tell you that this is the only way for them to get everything done.

In fact, the opposite is true. Multi-tasking is less productive. Sure, it makes sense to type a letter while you're waiting on hold on the telephone. Multi-tasking any more than that is deluding yourself. Recent research conducted at the University of Michigan studied patterns in the amounts of time lost when people switched repeatedly between two tasks of varying complexity and familiarity. The researchers found that participants lost time as they switched between tasks. The more complex the task, the more time was lost. And, the less familiar the task was, the more time was lost.

So if you're trying to respond to your e-mail, while dialing a phone number, drinking coffee, and filling out your expense form, you're likely to be less efficient, not more.

## Replace e-mail with meetings

Eliminate a flurry of e-mails flying back and forth by making your project meetings more productive. People dislike meetings because meetings tend to be poorly run. So they avoid them and use other ways to keep in touch. But there are times when meetings are more appropriate than any other form of communication. Use a meeting to:

- Become acquainted with team members
- Brainstorm ideas
- Plan complex projects

- Present and approve proposals
- Obtain consensus
- Provide brief updates on a project's status
- Motivate the team

There are times when a meeting is less appropriate. Don't use a meeting to:

- Solve problems that affect only one person's area
- Work out the details of a project
- Deal with individual personnel issues
- Provide detailed updates on a project's status
- Decide on a project's direction without sufficient information
- Edit written materials
- Get together just because you always do
- Plan an event from scratch
- Narrow down a long list of proposals (screen out the obvious duds beforehand)

Do you ever go to a meeting and ask yourself, "Why am I here? This is turning out to be a waste of my time. I wonder how I could get out of here?" Here's how to solve that problem. When someone invites you to a meeting via e-mail, don't agree to go unless you see an agenda. The agenda should include the start and end time, the location, a list of those invited, the subjects to be covered, the action items to be followed up and the decisions that will be made. If these aren't included, ask for them to be outlined in advance. If not, don't go.

## Take charge at meetings

The first rule for running meetings effectively is that anyone who attends can take responsibility for the meeting dynamics. If you're attending a poorly run meeting where you're not the chairperson, there's nothing stopping you from keeping the meeting on track. Here are some phrases you can use to exert control:

"When we wait for stragglers, we're rewarding those who come late and punishing those who made the commitment to be on time. Instead, why don't we just begin now?"

"Could we outline an agenda before we begin, so we know what we're covering?"

"We seem to be getting off track a bit. Should we get back to the matter at hand?"

"I've noticed our meetings have tended to run a little long. Is it possible we could set a finish time to keep us on track?"

"It seems that we haven't heard from a couple of people yet. I wonder if we can hear from them as well."

"That noise from outside is getting really loud. Could we move to a quieter room?"

"There are two conversations going on at the same time and it's difficult to keep track of all the good information I'm hearing. Could we have just one person speaking at a time?"

"I know voting will get us a firm decision, but I was wondering if there's a general consensus that seems to be emerging?"

"I'm a little unclear after that last discussion. Which alternative did we decide on?"
"Could we clarify who's going to follow up on the decision we just made?"
"Is someone taking notes to write up minutes afterwards?"
"Folks, we only have 15 minutes left and we still have three items to cover. Could we move things along a bit?"
"Just before we go, when and where will the next meeting be?"

## Send a handwritten note

E-mail works wonderfully for those brief business notes intended to convey quick messages. Friends and family also find e-mail keeps them more in touch than they ever were before. But never forget the handwritten note. You can make a statement with the card you buy or the stock you use. Your handwriting is a personal expression. The choice of ink reflects your mood, and the enclosures you send tell the reader that you took the time to care.

Write it by hand when it's a thank-you note, love letter, note of condolence, personal invitation, birthday card, note of appreciation or congratulation. As Joseph Addison said, "Words, when well chosen, have so great a force in them that a description often gives us more lively ideas than the sight of things themselves."

## Just say "no"

Say "no" to all those requests you're getting via e-mail. Many people say "yes" because they want to be liked or because they want to please others. But when they find themselves unable to meet their commitments, they let others down and feel guilty about it. Both parties suffer. You have a right to say "no." Remember that others will take you for granted and even lose respect for you if you don't.

To say "no," create a plan or a policy, and stick to it. ("Thanks, but I already have an investment plan, so you don't need to send me a newsletter about stocks.") When someone persists, repeat your position, perhaps in a slightly different way. ("As I already said, our policy is to donate to charities that help children only.")

Make sure you understand exactly what is being asked of you before you respond. Perhaps the task is more time-consuming than you thought. On the other hand, it may not take much effort at all.

Be polite, but firm in saying "no." You only build false hopes with wishy-washy responses. For instance, the phrase, "I'll try to be there," in response to a party invitation is giving yourself an excuse to avoid a commitment. It doesn't do anyone any favors.

When a superior asks you to take on an urgent task with a tight deadline, it's difficult to decline. What can you do?

- Remind him or her that you are working on other projects that have already been identified as top priorities.
- Ask for help in deciding where the new task should fall on the list of priorities.
- Ask, "What would you like to give up in order for me to do this?"
- Point out that you might be able to do everything, but not to the usual high standards that are expected.

When you say "no," some experts recommend keeping your answer short. This way, you can say "no" without feeling the need for a lengthy justification. ("I'm sorry, I'm not available that night.") On the other hand, others say that giving a longer answer with reasons reinforces your credibility. Let the situation decide.

## Say "yes, but..."

Sometimes you just can't say "no." For example, an urgent request comes your way via e-mail that has to get done. You're not too happy about it. Instead of griping though, say "yes" and take control of the situation rather than letting it take control of you. Provide suggestions or alternatives to the person who is asking. ("I can't do that task today, but how about next week?" or "I can help by finding out who should be doing this for you.")

Tell the person you can agree to the request this time, but ask how the two of you can plan better for the next time.

Tell the person you can do the task, but remind them they owe you one. For example, they might cover you for a shift next time you need time off.

Tell the person "yes," then take control by saying you'll come back with a timetable. For instance, "I expect I'll be able to do that for you by the end of the week." Put a tough condition on your agreement. "If it would only take an hour, I'd be able to help, but I can't give you more than that." When in doubt, it's easier to say "no" now, then change your mind to a "yes" later, rather than the other way around.

## Take a day off from e-mail

Do you remember those early advertisements for cellular phones, laptops, and handheld devices? People were lounging on the beach or sitting in an easy chair at the cottage with an electronic device in hand. There they were, casually tapping away, while sipping on a soda or massaging a mug of coffee. While they worked, a loving spouse looked on with a warm smile. You had to wonder, just because it was possible to do all that, who would want to? What would be the point of working while on vacation or on a weekend at the cottage? Sadly, that picture has become reality, except no one is smiling.

It's time to take a day off from e-mail. If you find yourself accessing your e-mail throughout the weekend, start with this experiment. Give yourself a day of rest from Saturday evening to Sunday evening (or perhaps one day earlier, depending on your religious faith). No e-mails, computers, faxes, pagers, or cellular phones. Just you and your family. Whether or not you are religious, spend one day away from work, including e-mail. You could go out to a movie, have dinner together, play in the park, or go for a walk. After dinner on Sunday evening, you could go back to work to prepare for the week, if you must. This won't cut back on the volume of e-mail, but it will give you more time for the things that matter.

# PUT YOUR IDEAS INTO ACTION

## Brainstorm new ideas

There are many more untapped ideas out there. Convene a team of three to seven people to conduct a brainstorming session on reducing e-mail. Brainstorming is a way to generate a large number of creative solutions to problems and it works because of synergy. A group's collective creativity results in ideas that no one person could have thought up. Productive brainstorming confirms the old adage that the whole is greater than the sum of the parts.

Meet in a quiet place away from distractions. When you're ready to start, clearly state the issue to be discussed, relevant background, and the desired outcome. Then it's time to go into full gear. Appoint someone to transcribe the ideas on a flip chart, and start asking for input. Use the four rules of brainstorming:

1. Quantity is desired, not quality. People should try to submit as many ideas as possible in rapid succession.
2. Postpone evaluative comments until later. Ask people to avoid phrases like "The boss won't allow that idea," or "There's no budget for that," or "That's not going to work because...."
3. Build on other ideas by hitchhiking. When someone suggests something, add onto his or her idea or find a new idea that connects with it in some way. Encourage participants to say, "That makes me think of something else...."

4. The more outrageous the ideas, the better. Just keep coming up with them and allow your imagination to go wild.

Beware of occasional violations of the second rule. Even phrases such as "We've listed that already," are a form of judgment and should be avoided. Try to control the order of speakers so that only one person speaks at a time. But if things get slightly unruly, let the energy flow and build. One person should transcribe the ideas. He or she will have difficulty keeping up with the volume, but that's to be expected. Writing ideas on a flip chart lets everyone see what's being said. A flip chart also allows you to type and circulate the results after the meeting.

An idea-generating session can be completed in 30 minutes. However, as you consider variations on the problem or as you look at other problems, you can capitalize on the group synergy and conduct a series of mini-sessions. So allocate enough time for the sessions. Include time for training, a warm-up exercise beforehand, and for evaluating ideas at the end.

---

## Measure progress

"If you can't measure it, you can't manage it." These wise words are from Peter Drucker, the famous management thinker. Consider measuring your own time, or the number of e-mails you receive. Conduct a snapshot study for a week or two to see how you're allocating your efforts. Don't do it for longer than that. You don't need yet another administrative activity to slow you down.

When you measure activities, create a yardstick that an outside objective observer could verify. For instance, your goal is not to feel better about e-mail or have fewer hassles with correspondence, as that would be too vague. Set a target to spend 20% less time on e-mail or to reduce complaints by 50%.

Also, conduct your measurements with a purpose in mind. Once you gather the data, what are you going to do with the findings? Convince your boss to change policies? Send out an e-mail with your results, thus adding to the glut? Or will you institute a personal policy about reducing the glut? Remember, it's not them – it's you.

## Be a champion of change

Change is never easy. Breaking an old habit and replacing it with a new one is a daunting task. For instance, simply resisting the idea of sitting down first thing in the morning and logging on to your e-mail will be tough to do. There can be all kinds of surprises and goodies in there. If you don't open them fast, they could disappear! Probably not, as you've discovered. Break the habit and take a few minutes to review your results, and plan your day before you rush into anything.

If you're having a tough time getting started, begin with one small change in behavior that can make a difference. Stop checking your e-mail messages so often. Limit the cc button. Get off distribution lists. Pick a date and time to start your change. Tell a co-worker or friend your plan to seal your commitment. Make your task concrete. It should be something you can check off at the end of the day and say, "Yes, I did that" (or "I didn't do that" as the case may be). Write down exactly what you'll do, or not do. Then stick to your plan.

Overcome procrastination by breaking large tasks into small pieces, by giving yourself a small reward for completing a task, and by visualizing your successful outcome.

Once you discover an idea that works, you'll want to let everyone else know. Of course, if they were convinced the idea was worth doing, they'd be doing it already. So you'll have an uphill battle convincing them. Lead by example. Show them your positive results. Expect skepticism. Be bold and be brave.

## Create balance

Now that you're spending much less time on e-mail, create more balance in your life. Many people confess that they really desire the things they're spending the least amount of time on. What do most people want time for? Fitness, community, family, friends, and learning. How about you?

Time for important things is all about choice. If you choose to make something important, and follow some fundamental productivity principles, you can achieve your desires – but maybe not all at once. If you've got a laundry list of wishes, you won't get to every one this year. But for now, choose one thing that you're hungry for. Then, set a goal, put time aside for it, and create a plan to make it happen. Making time for the things that count is not a luxury but a responsibility you have to yourself.

Find balance at work too. Work should be challenging and should push you, but it should also be fun. Strive to create an atmosphere of good humor buoyed by a positive attitude. Always make time for a proper lunch. Go for a short walk now and then to clear your mind of tensions. Leave your e-mail for a few hours. Taking a break will distract you from pressing problems and will create an opportunity for new ideas to incubate. Sometimes problems need to be left alone for a while.

Use humor at the office to maintain positive morale. That means sharing a joke in person, not just sending it via e-mail. Humor is a welcome antidote to an overwhelmingly frantic world. Attend social events with those on your team. The information you learn about them at the baseball game or the bar after work will help you understand them better.

Most of all, whether at work or home, keep smiling. Whatever challenges you face, the world will continue tomorrow. Throughout your life, remind yourself that you're in control of your time, and your reactions to all the craziness around you. You can create the life you want. Remember, your time is worth it.

## About the author

Mark Ellwood, president of Toronto-based Pace Productivity Inc., is an internationally known productivity consultant and the leading expert on how people spend their time. His company works with clients to identify and implement precise plans for employee improvement. A graduate of McGill University, he obtained a Bachelor of Commerce specializing in Organizational Behavior and Personnel in 1978. He invented the TimeCorder, a user-friendly device for tracking time spent on various activities. He is also the author of a book entitled *A Complete Waste of Time,* which combines humorous anecdotes with practical tips. He helps improve people and processes through consulting, training, and facilitation.

## Contact us

Visit our web site at www.GetMoreDone.com. You'll discover research reports, tips, and a unique interactive module called the Tabulator that allows you to create a time profile and compare it to others' profiles. You can reach Mark Ellwood, president of Pace Productivity Inc., for training and consulting, or to purchase additional copies of this book.

E-mail: mark@GetMoreDone.com
Phone: (416) 762-3453